THE FAT FIRM

The Transformation
of a Firm
from FAT to FIT

Andris Zoltners
Prabhakant Sinha
Stuart Murphy

Illustrations by Renée Williams–Andriani

Alex —

Thanks for your leadership
as we continue to get "FIT!!"

Ed Zell

9-8-98

McGraw-Hill

New York San Francisco Washington, D.C. Auckland Bogotá
Caracas Lisbon London Madrid Mexico City Milan
Montreal New Delhi San Juan Singapore
Sydney Tokyo Toronto

McGraw-Hill

A Division of The McGraw·Hill Companies

1 2 3 4 5 6 7 8 9 0   DOC/DOC   9 0 2 1 0 9 8 7

ISBN 0-07-044392-0

The sponsoring editor for this book was Susan Barry, the editing supervisor was Patricia V. Amoroso, and the production supervisor was Pamela Pelton.

Printed and bound by R.R. Donnelley & Sons Company.

This publication is designed to provide accurate and authoritative information in regard to the subject matter covered. It is sold with the understanding that the publisher is not engaged in rendering legal, accounting, or other professional service. If legal advice or other expert assistance is required, the services of a competent professional person should be sought.

> *—From a declaration of principles jointly adopted by a committee of the American Bar Association and a committee of publishers.*

McGraw-Hill books are available at special quantity discounts to use as premiums and sales promotions, or for use in corporate training programs. For more information, please write to the Director of Special Sales, McGraw-Hill, 11 West 19th Street, New York, NY 10011. Or contact your local bookstore.

To Greg, Jennifer, Angela, and Pat,
whose friendship I value greatly.

— A.A.Z.

To the women in my family —
Anita, Pria, Meera, and my Mother, for the joy and laughter.

— P.K.S.

To Nancy, Randy, and Maureen, and Kristin,
for their support.

—S.J.M.

For Vince,
who keeps our fat little corner of the world fit.

— R. W. A.

CONTENTS

ACKNOWLEDGMENTS

We would like to thank Greg Zoltners for the conceptual and editorial assistance he provided in the development of this book. Greg was constantly and enthusiastically scanning the business landscape for concepts that deserved a home in *The Fat Firm*.

We are grateful to Gary Facente, for being our guide and advisor about the world of publishing.

Linda Borcover put her formidable editorial talents to work. Not satisfied with inserting commas and straightening out sloppy phrases, she regularly challenged our ideas and images to enhance the book.

Linda Kluver worked tirelessly with the manuscript and cartoons through the numerous revisions of *The Fat Firm*. Just when she thought it was done, there was another page added, a cartoon revised, a concept deleted. Thank you, Linda, for your accuracy and your patience.

Nancy Smith successfully juggled her normal job and the erratic time demands of manuscript revision to help Linda Kluver. Thank you, Nancy, for pitching in with gusto and good humor.

We would also like to convey our thanks and apologies to the sea lions of the Galapagos Islands in Ecuador. The thanks are for inspiring the characters in the cartoons. The apologies are for using them as symbols of fat even though they are the essence of fitness.

We would also like to thank our families, friends, and colleagues, who were eager reviewers of successive versions of the concepts and cartoons used in this book.

We would like to thank Northwestern University's J.L. Kellogg Graduate School of Management and Rhode Island School of Design for providing fertile environments for ideas to flourish.

Finally, we would like to thank ZS Associates, a consulting firm that provided a laboratory for observing the business world and its people. The people of ZS contributed to the book through their creativity, and through their evaluation of our concepts. We also thank everyone at ZS for creating and maintaining an organization that is as fit as they come (we think), and a culture that will continue to maintain this fitness (we hope).

PART I

How Firms Get Fat

Everyone likes success. In business, success is measured by revenue and earnings growth, market share leadership, and customer satisfaction. We admire successful businesspeople, successful business cultures, and processes that produce high-margin, highly innovative products and services.

In addition to admiring business success, many strive for it and aspire to achieve it. Heads of companies want their companies to be global leaders. Managers want their products or their functional responsibilities to be the most productive in the firm. Stockholders want their investments to appreciate significantly. Business gurus want to develop the latest theory of the firm.

Today, businesspeople feel more and more pressure to succeed. Downsizing shifts work to fewer and fewer people. Intense competition reduces the opportunities for success. Stockholders ask for high returns on their investment. The media accentuate success and highlight failure.

Successful companies are scrutinized, and we celebrate their success formulas. We attempt to understand the determinants of success so that success can be replicated in other situations. Business cases and books are written describing effective management theories, methods, and tools.

We approach business success differently in this book. We suggest that success is hard work. There are no easy answers. Sure, a firm will win if it implements customer-focused strategies, constantly innovates, and attracts, grows, and retains top-quality people. But, then why doesn't every firm win? Because, success formulas do not apply equally well in every situation. They conflict at times, and there are millions of ways to implement them. What works in today's market environment with today's competitors may not work equally well tomorrow. The world is a dynamic place.

We celebrate business success in this book—we choose to call it fitness. We make fun of business mistakes—we call them "fat." Firms that make lots of errors are called "fat firms." We think that fitness can be achieved by understanding the sources of fat and developing the discipline to continuously eradicate it.

Fat occurs in three areas in the firm. It is stored in the firm's processes, is propagated by its culture, and is caused by its people. In this book, we demonstrate how people, culture, and processes create fat firms. By understanding fat, we learn how winners become winners and why winners stumble. In the end we show how the firm's people can change the firm's culture and its processes to achieve fitness.

The irony is that the seeds of failure are often found in success itself.

Most firms start out small and lean. Over time, some of them put on weight as they grow and prosper. To understand this process, it helps to look first at the activities that all firms perform and then at what fat firms do.

A firm
is comprised of people and a culture

that use money, technolgy, materials, and other resources

and develop business processes for innovation, manufacturing, marketing, and distribution

Product/Service Development:
R&D → Prototype → Launch
Distribution:
Factory → Wholesale → Retail → Customer
Customer Creation
Awareness → Trial → Repeat

to acquire customers and provide for their product or service needs

and consequently produce wealth, security, ego satisfaction, personal growth, and other benefits for the firm's employees and owners.

A fat firm
consists of people and a culture

that use too many resources

and employ unnecessary,
redundant, excessive, or
obsolete business processes,

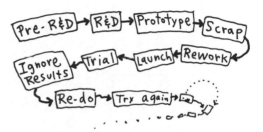

and thus, ultimately fail to
provide sustained value to
its customers

and place the employees' and
owners' wealth, security, ego
satisfaction, personal growth,
and other benefits at risk in
the future.

CHAPTER 1:
WHERE TO LOOK FOR FAT

People are at the heart of any firm. They shape the culture and
create the processes that harbor fat. The actions of the people can
display obvious fat—whether it be opulence, excessive spending,
or wasteful habits. But there is also less obvious fat such as
under-utilization of talent, energy spent on internal strife, and cultural resistance to change. The obvious is easy to see and remove,
if one has the will. But it takes insight to find the subtle forms of
fat and much more drastic measures to fix them.

We can look for fat in the leaders, the managers, and throughout
the firm.

It is obvious when a person in a position of authority spends lavishly on his surroundings. Opulent offices, a transportation fleet in waiting—these are some of the visible trappings of power, and they make a statement about a person's success and status. Many leaders squander human resources as well. They keep their people waiting and waste their time as they wait to see their leader.

Managers also contribute to fat. When a person uses the firm's resources for personal gain, the waste is evident since no benefit accrues to the firm or its customers. Often, this type of waste also becomes a mark of success.

In such situations, the culture itself gets corrupted as waste becomes everyone's habit. People actually aspire to the jobs that allow them to be wasteful spenders.

The firm's people take their cue from the managers and emulate the wasteful behaviors.

While the firm's leaders, managers, and other workers create fat through their wasted activities and spending, they can also create a more subtle form of fat. This possibly more dangerous form of fat can be found in a firm's attitudes, capabilities, and motivation.

An organization that strives to be good will never be excellent. Leaders who surround themselves with people who are weak or who rarely challenge them will never achieve excellence.

The firm's people create or inherit fat business processes. Process fat is often readily apparent and tends to be rectifiable. For years, the total quality movement has been enhancing processes. More recently, process redesign initiatives have captivated firms as they have attacked process waste in every domain. By addressing the more obvious forms of fat, these initiatives have usually produced leaner firms.

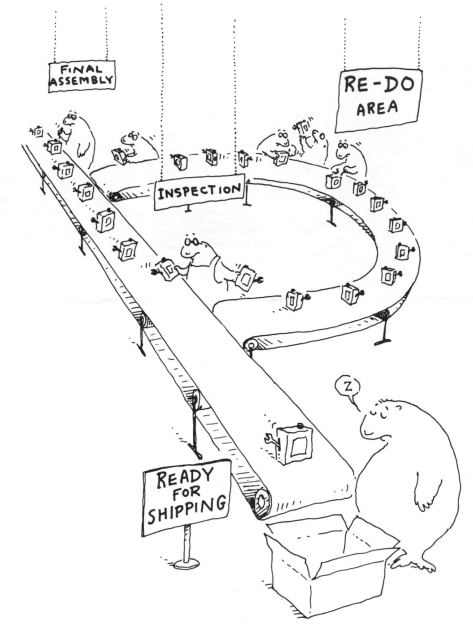

Processes sometimes become inefficient when they have strong process champions or when everyone feels that they have a need to know everything. The extra steps in such a process are clearly wasteful.

A more subtle form of fat occurs when the process incorporates suboptimal activities. Better activity choices may not be obvious to the process participants.

All processes need to be updated and improved over time. On occasion, process designers have difficulty in determining the right dimensions for change.

Finally, fat can be observed in the very fiber of the firm—in its culture. Cultures that accept inappropriate values or inspire wasteful workstyles will find it very difficult to get lean. Regrettably, culture fat can be difficult to spot, especially by the people within the culture.

"It's not coming out of my pocket!" is a prevalent attitude in the fat culture.

Cultures can emphasize individual performance or teamwork. Neither is right nor wrong—just appropriate or inappropriate for the current business environment. An inappropriate culture leads to ineffectiveness and fat.

CHAPTER 2:
HOW AND WHY FIRMS GET FAT

Some firms get fat. Others stay lean. There are common traits shared by all firms that explain how and why some get fat or continue to stay fat. Four simple principles capture most of the causes.

1.   **Environment:** The environment gives some firms more opportunities to get fat than others.

2.   **Predisposition:** Individuals have a natural predisposition for survival, success, and pleasure, and thus create fat in a firm.

3.   **Easy choice:** Getting fat is the easy choice.

4.   **Increasing entitlement:** Once fat takes hold it becomes a habit that is hard to break.

Favorable Environments Encourage Fat

Every firm interacts with customers, potential customers, competitors, suppliers, government, and society. Every firm faces changing customer needs, recessions and expansions, technical shifts, fluctuating capital markets, evolving social values, and even natural disaster. At times these elements create a beneficial environment for the firm—the economy is booming, the customers love the firm's products, the competitors are weak, and money is cheap. When favorable environments persist for sustained periods of time the firm enjoys significant opportunities to succeed. But success may hold the seeds of its own undoing, including the opportunity to get fat.

The environment that any firm experiences can be profiled on a continuum from unfavorable to favorable.

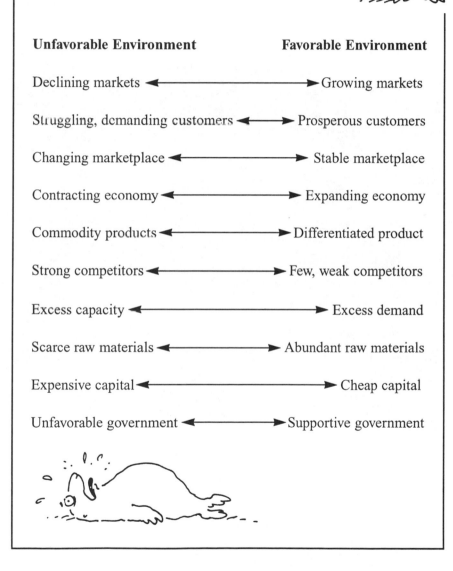

"High-Fat opportunities"

Unfavorable Environment   **Favorable Environment**

Declining markets ←————————→ Growing markets

Struggling, demanding customers ←——→ Prosperous customers

Changing marketplace ←————————→ Stable marketplace

Contracting economy ←————————→ Expanding economy

Commodity products ←————————→ Differentiated product

Strong competitors ←————————→ Few, weak competitors

Excess capacity ←————————————→ Excess demand

Scarce raw materials ←————————→ Abundant raw materials

Expensive capital ←————————————→ Cheap capital

Unfavorable government ←————————→ Supportive government

People's Needs Lead to Fat

The fulfillment of people's desires and aspirations can create fat in a firm. In our society, we desire large incomes, exciting leisure activities, recognition, and power—the trappings of the good life. In fact, these very things define success. We expect our firms to help us realize these dreams and aspirations.

A fit firm is able to establish the line between individual motivation and company excess. When the welfare of the individual begins to dominate the welfare of the company, fat can set in.

Easy Work Causes Fat

We make decisions every day. Sometimes we choose to do easy work. Sometimes we choose to do hard work. Easy work makes life more enjoyable and reduces stress. However, too much easy work can lead to mediocrity, lack of competitiveness, wasteful habits, redundant processes–fat.

EASY WORK:

DELIVERY

Spend Money

Hire Someone

Give a Big Raise

Buy Something

Tolerate Customer

Pay Full Price

Stay the Same

Make It Good Enough

Increase Staff

HARD WORK:

Save Money

Fire Someone

Give No Raise

Sell Something

Delight Customer

Negotiate Lower Price

Get Better

Make It Exceptional

Increase Productivity

Fat Escalates Over Time

An earlier principle says that individuals have a predisposition for survival, success, and enjoyment. This principle suggests that yesterday's rewards become tomorrow's expectations, and that once fat takes hold it becomes hard to deny it and very easy to introduce more. Individuals change in a successful firm. Their expectations increase; they want more and more. Entitlement creeps into the firm's culture, and the culture develops an entitlement momentum that is powerful enough to sweep along all of the firm's people. The firm becomes entitled to its fat.

CHAPTER 3:
THE DYNAMICS OF THE FAT FIRM

For most firms, the process of getting fat tends to follow a predictable pattern.

The environment, individual aspirations, people's attraction to easy work, and increasing entitlement lead to a predictable evolutionary pattern. The dynamics of the fat firm can be easily visualized if we think of two types of environments—favorable and unfavorable—and two types of firms—fat and fit. This combination leads to four situations:

TYPES OF FIRMS

FIT:
TOUGHY is a fit firm in a favorable environment.

FAT:
COMFY is a fat firm in a favorable environment.

ENVIRONMENTS   FAVORABLE: UNFAVORABLE:

SCRAPPY is fit in an unfavorable environment.

IFFY is fat in an unfavorable environment.

Firms don't remain static in these situations. If a firm is doing well because of a rapidly expanding market or a lack of competition, it attracts competitors and the game is bound to get harder. If the firm is fit in a favorable environment, the lure of easy work is strong. Fat sets in. No matter where a firm lies on this fitness-fatness spectrum or how favorable or unfavorable the environment, predictable things happen.

Let's begin with TOUGHY, a fit firm in a favorable environment. Through ingenuity and effort, it is doing well, and the environment helps feed its success. New customers fuel growth. The best people want to join the firm and experience its culture of success.

Capital is plentiful as Wall Street feeds thehot hand. Customers praise the firm's innovation and service. TOUGHY's discipline keeps all eyes on the business, all costs in line. The future looks bright.

But success has its dangers. Raises increase at a faster rate than productivity gains each year. People seek and get more support and staff. Offices become a little more luxurious. Spending discipline becomes harder and harder to maintain. Mediocrity is tolerated as easy work becomes the norm. The favorable environment also encourages easy work, so business processes are only marginally upgraded. As the firm's affluence is transferred to the firm's leaders and managers, the value of leisure increases throughout the leadership, then the firm. People lose the edge born of hunger. They make investments because money is available, not because the projects add value. TOUGHY is easing into the COMFY stage.

People in the COMFY firm are, feel, and look successful. The business press lauds COMFY's success. People have few worries as the innovation and hard work of the past continues to reward the firm with sales and profits. Easy work prevails in a still favorable environment.

But this environment doesn't continue forever. It becomes harder and harder to replicate prior product and market successes. COMFY—self-indulgent, overpriced, inefficient, comfortable with easy work—is ill-equipped to deal with the emergence of nimble and hungry competitors. Once-loyal customers look elsewhere for cheaper, higher-quality, and more responsive sources. Managers in the COMFY firm cling to obsolete strategies and blame their leaders. Top performers dust off their resumes and look for other opportunities. COMFY has become IFFY, fat in an unfriendly environment.

What becomes of IFFY? It faces either a fitness regimen based on hard work or it faces death. To survive, IFFY has to change company habits and culture and people's attitudes and actions. It has to consume less and produce more. If it completes this painful transformation, IFFY becomes SCRAPPY, the fit firm in an unfavorable environment.

SCRAPPY's survival depends on iron-willed persistence and staying fit through relentless hard work. Discipline is the best tactic. But even an unfriendly environment can provide opportunity: it may weed out competitors. With any luck, a determined firm may survive while some of its competitors disappear. In time, with effort, SCRAPPY could find itself fit in an improving environment. But will the cycle begin again?

COMFY is the epitome of the fat firm. The financial results are good. Employee morale is high. Stockholders are pleased. However, the firm is getting internally focused. Complex processes and systems are created to support other internal processes and systems. The voice of the customer is heard only faintly, if at all.

It takes a while for the financial results to catch up to the realities of undisciplined fat behavior. Amidst the internal celebration, the customer's observations about the firm's fading glory are lost. Even when the news does come, there can be denial and anger before the acceptance of reality. How did it happen? The firm's people, culture, and processes provide the answers.

PART II

How People Create Fat

The waste, redundancy, and inefficiency of a fat firm conjure up images of a bloated business that can be fixed only by reducing its size and redesigning its processes. Downsizing, delayering, out-sourcing, and business process redesign are common prescriptions for fixing fat. But these medicines are only part of the answer. A fundamental place to look for fat in a firm is in its people. The people are the drivers that produce business outcomes. Central to the understanding of a fat firm is the understanding of its people.

People are at the center of any firm. People's behaviors produce beneficial effects-processes, systems, activities, customer relation-ships, sales, and profitability. But their behaviors have the poten-tial to produce detrimental effects as well.

Both the number of people (the quantity) and their effectiveness (the quality) affect the amount of fat in a firm. Unfortunately, firms often measure fat by considering quantity alone. This is understandable since quantity is observable and recognizable; a firm can see that it has 50 or 5,000 employees. Quality is subtle and more difficult to measure. Many firms have downsized in an effort to cut fat and achieve greater success. But quality improve-ment often has a greater impact on a company's prosperity.

The activities that people perform and how well they perform them determine the firm's success. The firm prospers when its people do their jobs well, whether by treating customers properly, setting direction, working cooperatively, or creating a positive environment and value system.

The quality of these activities is largely caused by a few potent forces.

- Motivators, which are basic human drives that induce action
- Values, which are principles or standards that shape behavior
- Attitudes, which consist of a person's feelings, thinking, and disposition
- Capabilities, which include the skill and knowledge needed to successfully perform within the firm

Capabilities, values, and attitudes capture what people can do and who they are, while motivators drive people to action. Together, these forces lead to behaviors that may or may not be consistent with the firm's objectives. Fat occurs when these central forces create behaviors that may help an individual while damaging the interests of the firm. The firm is most successful when the forces that govern the actions of its people are aligned with the firm's well-being.

and Attitudes

Capabilities

CHAPTER 4:
MOTIVATORS

People are motivated by a few basic needs. The survival instinct ensures human existence by helping people deal with competitive threats, a hostile environment, and demanding customers. Social affiliation gives people a feeling of belonging, the sense that they are accepted and liked, and binds the people in the firm into a cohesive group. The need to achieve contributes to the creation of successful products, processes, and systems. The power motivator helps people control others and the environment. It facilitates decision making and ensures that the firm has strong leaders. Finally, ego gratification satisfies the need for pride and self-esteem.

Success results when these motivational forces are strong and aligned with the firm's objectives. However, motivators that are too weak or misdirected can lead to inefficiency and fat. For example, if the firm's people are complacent and lack the will to achieve, it will not be long before they are no longer responsive to market conditions and are overrun by the competition. Individuals with intense needs can create internal strife and anxiety or be self-serving, putting themselves ahead of the firm and its customers.

Survival

The need to survive motivates everyone. The survival instinct is triggered when individuals perceive that their jobs are endangered by external or internal threats. External threats arise when competition intensifies, key customers threaten to move their business, or environmental forces change the way the firm needs to compete. Internal threats occur when jobs are eliminated, responsibilities are reduced, and familiar job activities are changed. These threats can be caused by such factors as internal competition, reorganization, process redesign, or technology upgrading. Interestingly, people seem to take notice of internal threats more frequently than external threats.

An individual's survival instinct can help or hinder the firm, depending on whether or not the individual's survival behavior is aligned with the firm's objectives. The firm prospers if a person's survival motivation leads to actions that overcome the threat to the individual and benefit the firm at the same time. This can happen when a person's behavior enhances the firm's ability to deal with strong competitive threats, adapt to environmental changes, and focus on customer needs. Manufacturing processes get enhanced in response to low-cost competitors. Salespeople strive harder when a competitor threatens their key accounts.

On the other hand, individual survival behavior can be misaligned with the objectives and strategies that ensure the firm's well-being.

When a force such as new technology threatens familiar activities, an individual with a misdirected survival instinct will fight the threat.

If power, position, or responsibilities are reduced, people naturally tend to put their personal interests ahead of the firm's.

When jobs are threatened, people instinctively try to fight the job loss and survive.

They lobby, build coalitions, gatekeep, and otherwise attempt to block the threat for their own benefit.

The firm can cause a misdirected survival response. When people are in the wrong job or when the company's demands on people are excessive, the survival motivator will kick in.

Fat can also be the result of a weak or dulled survival instinct. Some people naturally lack strong survival motivation, and the work environment can weaken this motivator in others. If a person has to constantly deal with environmental changes, demanding customers, and competitive peers, the survival instinct is likely to be aroused constantly and reinforced regularly. But if the firm consistently shields its people from anxiety, the survival instinct dulls. In time, a weak survival instinct can lead to fat in a firm.

Social Affiliation

Everybody needs and wants to be liked and appreciated. Social affiliation binds the people of a firm to each other and to their customers and suppliers. It is a source of empathy and sensitivity. It helps create and maintain customer relationships. The need for social affiliation facilitates and sustains teamwork. It enables and enhances coaching and leads to harmonious interaction among peers and among people at different levels in a firm. But, as with the other motivators, too much misdirected social affiliation or too little social affiliation can cause fat in organizations.

Individuals with an exaggerated need for social affiliation may want to do things that win them even more acceptance and appreciation—even if their actions hurt the firm.

The person with a hunger for social affiliation may avoid giving a subordinate negative feedback.

When a person with a strong need for social affiliation is part of a team, he will hold back valid but conflicting opinions for fear of hurting other people. Even in dealing with customers, too much social affiliation can be a source of inefficiency and fat.

A salesperson may discount excessively in order to maintain a relationship.

A person with a weak need for social affiliation doesn't work hard enough to be liked and is often insensitive to the needs of others. Such a person can create an atmosphere of fear among subordinates and bring strife and friction to teams.

Achievement

Most successful people are achievement oriented, and their push for personal success creates winning products, processes, and firms. It is easy to see how a lack of desire for achievement can hurt a firm. Complacency replaces the desire to improve. In the global economy and with fierce competition in every domain, no competitive edge is sustainable without a healthy mix of paranoia and the achievement motivator.

At the same time, a strong but misdirected achievement motivator can also produce fat in a firm. When people's desire to achieve is directed away from the interests of the firm, the achievement motivator that is so essential for fit firms becomes a force for fat.

R&D Scorecard

Publications 7 2

Patents 8

Products 0

Even when the focus is on products or results, zealous overdesign can result from an overly strong achievement motivator combined with a lack of attention to market needs.

When trying to achieve at all costs, a person may succeed, but do so at the expense of customers and other people in the firm   For example, a salesperson can sell a product that the customer does not need or that the company cannot produce or deliver. When there is too much internal competition, a person may withhold information from colleagues to hinder their achievement. A manager may hoard all of the recognition for the job done by the team.

While misdirected achievement creates fat in indirect ways, lack of desire for achievement is a much more obvious source of fat. It results in disinterest, lethargy, and complacency—all of which lead to stagnation.

Lack of achievement can manifest itself as a lack of confidence, an attitude of negativism or laziness.

Power

Firms face a wide range of decisions. The choices they make affect their people, determine their processes, and establish their culture. People make these decisions for the firm—people in power control the choices.

Individual power can be obtained through ownership, position, expertise, or charisma. The positive use of power in a firm moves the firm forward. Decisions are made quickly. Appropriate use of power gives a group direction and cuts through ambiguity and needless dissension. On the other hand, power abuse or an ongoing struggle for power can divert the firm's energy. Coercion, manipulation, and control through dictatorial behavior and empire building can improve the status of the individual, but weaken the firm.

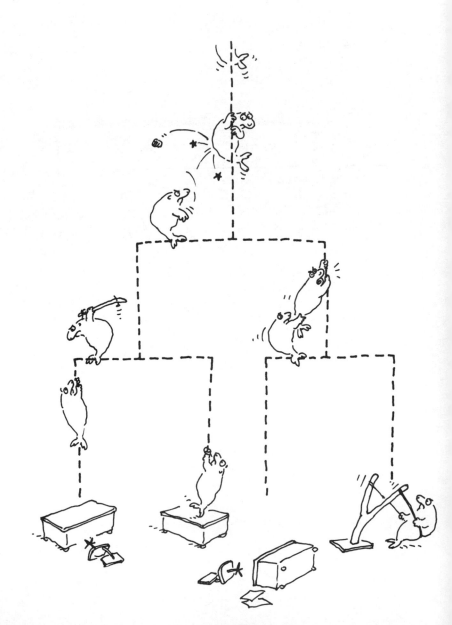

Power can be misused in many ways. For example, people in positions of power can put self-interest ahead of the company. They use power to push through decisions that help themselves at the expense of the firm.

A powerful person manipulating weaker people is an obvious example of a power motivator gone awry. A more subtle form is when a person seeks to sustain power by surrounding himself with weaker people. When strength is perceived to be a threat by the firm's decision makers, then weakness will undoubtedly become the firm's norm.

The gatekeeper uses his position to control information, processes, or people. This obvious misuse of power does not create any value for the firm. Bureaucracies of every kind are adept at creating gatekeepers who do nothing but sap an organization's energy.

Monopolies and near-monopolies can create situations in which their customers feel the brunt of a misdirected power motivator. A victimized customer lacks choice and is powerless to do anything in the near-term. In this situation, the customer will constantly look for substitutes, encouraging the growth of competitors.

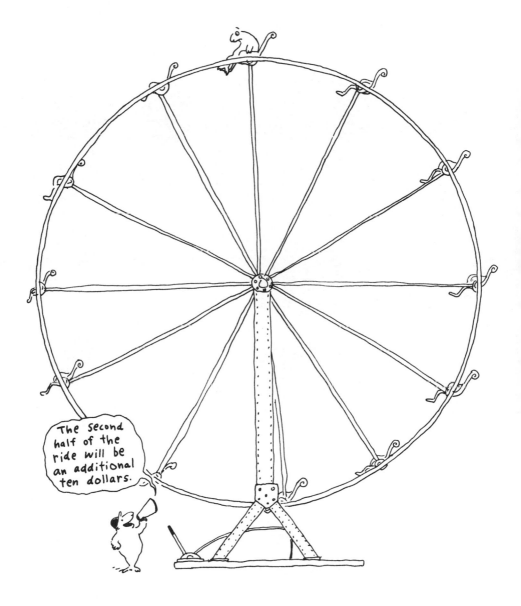

Abuses of power have detrimental effects on the firm. An inadequate supply of the power motivator will cause different kinds of problems. The firm will flounder and be indecisive. Slow decisions and uncoordinated activities will be the norm.

Ego Gratification

People naturally have ego drive. When the need for achievement is satiated, the ego motivator can provide a force that keeps individuals striving. In the best circumstances, both employee and firm benefit.

Trophies communicate accomplishment and embody recognition. They feed the individual ego. But, their attainment can sometimes create a distraction from the firm's mission. When this happens, the firm gets a little fatter.

An excessively strong, misdirected ego drive can conflict with the firm's best interests. The firm misuses valuable inputs when its people use the firm's money and time to feed their egos without any compensating productivity gains.

References in books, university case studies, and business press articles indicate that a firm and its leaders are successful. They feed the corporate ego.

These public relations efforts are successful when they strengthen the firm's ties with its employees, customers, and investors, and demoralize the competition. However, publicity can also create unwanted results, such as better trained competition, demoralized employees, and customers with information they can use to negotiate better deals.

An overbearing ego and poor listening skills are a dangerous mixture. Other people's ideas never get a chance to succeed.

1.

2.

3.

4.

Too little ego-drive can have undesirable consequences as well. Good ideas never see the light of day.

CHAPTER 5:
VALUES AND ATTITUDES

People's values and their attitudes toward their companies, their jobs, and their peers can mean the difference between an organization's success and failure. Positive, highly motivated groups that share a constructive value system are high-performance groups. At the same time, the combination of a poor attitude and a negative value system is a catalyst for disaster. Neither properly aligned motivators nor great capabilities can compensate for this force. Poor values and negative attitudes divert energies from the work at hand.

Individual values and attitudes can be observed by watching how employees treat their customers, their peers, and their company. Integrity, quality consciousness, and fairness are three dimensions for viewing individual values. Attitudes build on these values, and are an expression of individual feelings and opinions. Employees with negative values and attitudes contribute their share of fat to the firm.

Integrity

Uprightness, honesty, and sincerity are valued by society. The lack of these values sometimes leads to individual success, but it can come at the expense of others.

If a group doesn't value integrity, individuals will sometimes let honesty slip—at the expense of their customers, their peers, or their firm.

Integrity allows trust to develop, and trust is essential for an organization to work cooperatively together and with its customers.

Quality

Striving for and achieving excellence is essential for a firm to maintain high market share and high margins and continue to grow. Quality enhancement programs are now firmly ingrained in the fabric of most well-defined processes. In referring to quality here, the focus is on values and not processes. A person who values quality will seek to continuously improve himself, his firm's products and services, and the processes that involve him. It is quality consciousness at this organic level that will lead to breakthroughs. This kind of individual quality focus is required if a firm is to improve and revitalize its business processes in the face of changing customer needs and unpredictable environmental forces.

Quality enhancement is hard work. Rationalization is easy work.

Fairness

Fairness contributes to harmony in a firm. People who feel that they are treated fairly have high job satisfaction, which ultimately leads to job involvement and the effective utilization of talent. Selfishness can create serious inefficiencies. Employee conflict may arise, teamwork can become impossible, and work may not get done.

By their very nature, firms bring people together to achieve common goals. Goals are sometimes clear and sometimes ambiguous. Unlike athletic environments where goals and roles are very clear, business environments are more ambiguous. Fairness is a key value in ambiguous environments. As anyone who has been part of a work team knows, teams can create significant synergy when they work harmoniously. Teams flounder when one or more members seek individual credit and achievement at the expense of the group or when some members are free riders.

Just as too much self-interest causes fat, too much self-sacrifice also causes fat, because the skills and energies of the entire team are not fully used.

Attitudes

All people have feelings and opinions, and they continuously update them. An individual's attitude concerning his firm will affect his behavior and performance. When shared, his feelings will affect the behavior and performance of others as well.

Employees tend to stay tuned to the daily events of the firm. The firm can have ups and downs, act properly, or make mistakes. These events are observed and communicated. Attitudes are formed. At times these attitudes can swing significantly. Most firms have periods of low morale. Productivity suffers when negative attitudes prevail for long periods of time across groups within the workforce.

CHAPTER 6:
PERSONAL CAPABILITIES

People in a firm play different roles in order to be successful. A specific job will typically use a mixture of leadership, management, and execution skills.

Individuals with leadership ability are able to develop a clear vision, shape a successful firm strategy, select people wisely, affirm values, communicate, persuade, evoke confidence, and create excitement. People who manage effectively build a team, define and organize work, delegate, empower, motivate, coach, and monitor. Those who execute well get the job done in a timely, efficient, high-quality manner. Motivation, good values, and a good attitude are essential ingredients, but they are not sufficient. Capabilities complete the picture.

Individuals within the firm utilize each of these capabilities to varying degrees. The relative importance of these capabilities depends on where people are in their careers, how the firm is organized, and the external market environment. For example, a product development team may need all these capabilities to differing degrees in each of its members. It needs a vision and a strategy, which require leadership. It needs to define and organize its work, which require management skills. It needs execution skills to get the tasks done. The organizational structure, whether flat, hierarchical, or cross-functional, only changes the balance of the capabilities required from each person. All of the capabilities are needed to succeed.

The lack of personal capabilities shows up in two important ways. Individuals may lack the knowledge to accomplish their jobs. For example, a salesperson may not know his product line or his customer's needs very well. An operations supervisor may not know how to manage a production process, material flows, or inventory. Alternatively, individuals may not have the skills to accomplish their jobs. A salesperson may know his products, customer needs, and the mechanics of selling, but may not be able to apply this knowledge. He leaves most sales calls not knowing why he did not get the business. An operations supervisor may know the mechanics of his job but be unskilled at scheduling, motivating people, and crisis management. People's lack of personal capabilities leads to firm-wide fat.

Leadership

In this age of empowerment and horizontal organizational structures, firms demand leadership skills from everyone. As jobs give way to roles, a person may need to be the leader on one team, a manager on another, and a worker on a third.

A firm with poor leadership stumbles along. Leaders who have no vision, an ambiguous vision, or a flawed vision cannot develop a successful strategy for the firm or a subgroup within the firm. People will not align behind such a leader, and the firm is left floundering.

Go this way!
Over here!
No, this way!
This way!
This way!
Over here!
CEO
Five dollars says he'll have more production offshore and increase executive pay.
I'll bet we downsize next month.
Ten dollars says he'll take a three-hour lunch!
A hundred dollars says it'll be more than 15%!

A good leader needs both internal and external knowledge to set direction. Externally, he may need to be very familiar with the dynamics of the industry, the needs of the customers, the environment, economic trends, competition, technology trends, and innovative management practices.

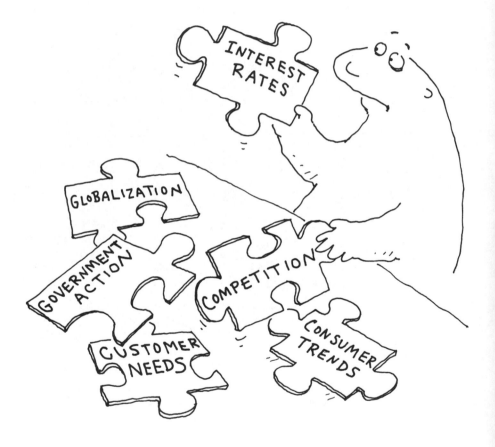

Internally, the leader needs to know his people and the strengths and weaknesses of the firm as well as the key business processes. Lacking a good knowledge of the firm's core competencies, the leader may try to implement initiatives that are not feasible.

Leaders need the skill to absorb, distill, and integrate signals from the team and the environment. Without this ability, the vision and strategy for the firm may be vacuous.

A good leader is a good communicator. His strategy is expressed clearly and it becomes shared by the organization. His communication skills mobilize the team to achieve a shared vision. Poor communication skills create uncertainty and misdirection.

Leadership is a human activity. Ninety percent of a leader's time is spent with others. The leader builds trust and commitment. The poor leader fails to bring out the best in his people.

Leadership skills are best honed in crises. Therefore, it is often difficult to reliably predict who the best leaders will be, and candidates without good leadership skills frequently end up in leadership rolls. If these individuals fail to perform their roles effectively, the firm can only underachieve. Regrettably, the negative results of a poor leader sometimes lag behind his actions by months or even years.

Management

Individuals who manage are charged with achieving the firm's objectives through the efforts of others. The successful manager forms the right team, builds its competencies, and makes sure that the firm's objectives are achieved.

Individuals who manage poorly multiply the fat in a firm. Not only are they ineffective themselves, but the entire team becomes ineffective as well.

Selection, role definition, development, and deselection are all components of success when it comes to assembling a team. Selecting inappropriate or incompetent team members is the sign of a poor manager. Defining the wrong role for a team member is a form of fat. Keeping incapable people too long reduces productivity as well.

Good managers build the team's competence and grow their people. They challenge team members, encourage self-development, train, coach, counsel, provide feedback, measure progress and support their team members. A poor manager's team atrophies over time.

Good managers establish good working relationships with team members. They are open. They listen well. They have professional discussions with the team. They define clear roles, responsibilities, and objectives. They delegate and empower appropriately. They communicate company strategy, policy, and events. Individuals tend to be poor managers when they micromanage, try to do everything themselves, behave inconsistently, or are indecisive.

A good manager is a good motivator and creates a positive work environment by being fair and interested. The manager recognizes the team's accomplishments and rewards appropriately. A manager who is thoughtless, unfair, unethical, takes undue credit, plays political games, or overworks the team will create poor morale and a dysfunctional team.

A good manager sets and exceeds high performance standards. He increases productivity continuously. He controls expenses and allocates resources. He communicates company values and provides feedback to other parts of the organization so that overall organizational decision making is enhanced. Individuals who do not have the knowledge or skills to accomplish these tasks are likely to be poor managers. Frequently, people get promoted until they reach their level of incompetence.

Execution

The firm needs people who can do the work expeditiously and well. It needs people who have the skills and knowledge to execute its tasks and processes capably. In the fit firm, talented people are hired and their capabilities are developed. Experience, along with an organizational and individual learning process, prepares people for their future jobs. Inadequate knowledge and skills can be due to poor selection, poor development, or the inability to adapt to changing market needs.

The execution of the firm's work is only as good as the people who are doing the work.

Gazette

Chief Executive Officer Edward Zwick announces the following promotions:

John S. Zwick
Vice President,
Operations

Dave Zwick
General Manager,
New Products
Division

Natalie
Zwick-Bumpus
Director of
Purchasing

Hank Zwick
Vice President,
Research and Development

Beverly Zwick
Vice President,
Market Research

SUMMARY

When firms try to reduce fat, they may try strategies such as downsizing, organizing around small business teams, and empowerment. But they need to begin by understanding the people of the firm—their motivators, capabilities, and values. Strategies that deal only with quantity and size are often superficial. Fat can return as soon as there is modest business improvement, because the causes of fat run very deep. Fat is a consequence of people's basic motivators, their capabilities, and their value systems. And that's where real change needs to begin.

PART III

The Culture
of the Fat Firm

People have motivators, capabilities, and values. But a firm has a personality too—its culture. The culture can be thought of as the genes of the firm. The culture guides the firm's people as they continuously encounter familiar or new situations. The culture establishes a baseline for the firm's decision making and for its acceptable behaviors.

Groups within the firm can have their own subcultures. For example, a sales force may celebrate individualism, while the development team embraces teamwork. A customer service department's priority is the customer, while the human resource department focuses on the people of the firm. Some cultural elements, such as the importance of seniority or performance, may be common across the firm, whereas others are tailored to the objectives of a group within the firm.

CHAPTER 7:
THE ELEMENTS OF CULTURE

The firm's culture consists of its values and is reflected in its workstyle. Culture is communicated through the firm's heroes, legends, celebrations, and rewards. When a firm rewards an innovation it makes a statement about what it values. A story about a person's initiative on behalf of a customer is repeated in glowing terms. A person's failed investment in a new market segment is examined, understood, and becomes part of the corporate experience. These are all manifestations of company culture.

The firm's values specify what is important. They are the principles and standards that guide behavior. Frequently, values are seen in the way the firm resolves its conflicts and dilemmas. For example, who is more important: the firm's people or the firm's customers? Which is less desirable: that an employee work 80 hours in a week or that a customer waits a week longer for a part?

The firm's workstyle can be seen in the nature of the everyday activities of its employees. Workstyle refers to how people act, how they make decisions, how they interact with each other, and how they interact with customers. The workstyle can be organic, encouraging creativity, flexibility, and spontaneity, or it can be mechanical, encouraging control, order, and inflexibility. Individualism or teamwork can be rewarded. Workstyles can be autocratic or consensual; they can be empathetic or cutthroat. The workstyle can emphasize an external focus on the competition and market environment or it can look internally to integration and smooth working relationships.

Cultures are formed by the firm's history, environment, and people. A firm's culture evolves. The firm's people continually redefine the culture. Their current motivators, capabilities, values, and attitudes drive their current decisions, actions and behaviors, which in turn, refashion the culture.

A powerful, ego-driven leader or a strong subgroup can have an immediate impact on the firm's culture. Prominent individuals with strong achievement or social affiliation motivators can move cultures in these directions. Highly capable employees with positive attitudes can enhance the firm's culture, while employees with few capabilities or a poor attitude will diminish the culture.

The culture is anchored in the firm's history and is the cumulative result of prior decisions and actions. Cultural components that contribute to a firm's success get reinforced. If teamwork leads to success, it can become a cultural norm. The firm's culture attracts compatible people and rejects nonconformists. Culture shapes its people, even as its people are shaping culture.

External events such as changing customer needs, competitive actions, legislation, and even nature's gifts or disasters shape cultures. Cultures that adapt quickly are successful while those that overlook these externalities may be ill-equipped to deal with the future.

Favorable environments create opportunities for business success, which in turn provides the climate for a fat culture to form. People succeed and are rewarded. Yesterday's reward becomes tomorrow's entitlement. This leads to fat and the inevitable trauma of downsizing when the environment turns unfriendly.

Cultures become fat when they support individual needs at the expense of the firm or when they are incompatible with a new environment. A successful firm can easily become smug and choose easy work at the expense of product innovation and customer satisfaction. A culture is incompatible with the environment when it is organized functionally and its customers are demanding cross-functional teams, or when a dated workstyle employs structured and well-defined tasks and the marketplace requires creativity, flexibility, and adaptability.

CHAPTER 8:
THE VALUES OF THE FIRM

A culture makes statements about how customers, employees and company assets are to be treated. These statements reveal what is important to the firm. A common cultural dilemma is the relative importance of the customer, the people, and the firm itself. In an era of constant downsizing and restructuring, a clear cultural statement is being made that the firm is more important than the people.

Statements About Customers

All firms rely on meeting customer needs in order to generate revenues and profits and keep their people employed. The firm succeeds if its customers succeed. But not all firms, even within the same industry, treat their customers the same way. Some understand their customers better than others. Some are more innovative than others. Some are more service-oriented than others. Some are more empathetic and ethical than others. The culture makes a statement about how much the firm values its customers. The fat firm's culture does not place enough value on its customers.

A culture that is too internally focused will have difficulty understanding its customers and servicing their needs. Cultures that do not listen to customers or are too casual when it comes to understanding and satisfying their needs, will slowly see their customers disappear.

Customer focus, customer satisfaction, and customer delight are central cultural themes for many firms. However, a firm in a monopolistic situation, or a firm with a product line having a significant differential advantage, can easily make a cultural choice that places the firm and the people ahead of the customers. Prices go up, margins escalate, service is reduced, and responsiveness declines. Where is the customer?

What is said and done under the guise of customer focus may only serve the short-term interests of the fat firm.

Internal focus can also take the form of process focus, where rules and procedures dominate. These procedures can conflict with the best interests of the customer. Often the rigidity of a highly process-driven firm runs counter to the best interests of the people and the firm as well.

The self-interest of a firm or the self-interest of the firm's people can at times cross the line of ethics. Unethical behavior sometimes produces short-term gains, but can never succeed in the long-term. It is a myopic strategy. It ultimately creates resentment, erodes customer loyalty, and encourages switching at the first available opportunity.

Statements About Employees

A firm's culture sets norms for how people will be treated. The firm may respect its employees and celebrate their successes or it may exploit them to generate higher profits.

Cultural norms can have a profound effect on the firm. They help determine who gets hired, how over- and underperformers are defined, and how peers and multiple levels within the organization will interact. Cultural norms also affect how career paths, development programs, motivational programs, and employee incentives are established. They establish the cohesiveness of the organization. Mistakes on these dimensions create fat for the firm.

A key source of employee motivation is appreciation. When supervisors are asked what their subordinates want from their jobs, they suggest high pay and job security as the top priorities, and place their subordinates' need for appreciation and interesting work well down the list. Meanwhile, when subordinates are asked what they desire most in their jobs, they rank appreciation and interesting work before money and security. This apparent disconnect in values leads to cultures that do not value people enough.

Another key motivator is empowerment. A firm that consistently fails to empower its people creates an environment where people are underutilized. They feel that they have little control over their work, that their capabilities are underemployed, and that they could be contributing much more to the success of the firm. This leads to eventual stagnation. Too little empowerment weakens a firm.

But there is such a thing as too much empowerment. Sometimes people do not have the skills, knowledge, or experience to complete a given task. Empowering the wrong people or providing empowerment without sufficient training or a clear direction can hurt the individual as well as the firm. Unsuccessful employees lose motivation and have low levels of job satisfaction. They also lose credibility among their peers and supervisors.

All firms need to provide interesting, challenging, and motivating work for their people. But cultures that set unrealistic expectations for their employees and continually press for more and more effort and output will finally push expectations beyond anyone's capacity.

A valued person is appreciated and empowered. But a person needs to grow as well. Some cultures buy stars, others build them. People do not develop in cultures where learning is not the norm. People are better able to succeed in their jobs and grow in their careers if the firm provides opportunities for personal development, and where people are personally and culturally driven to exploit these opportunities.

Employees do not grow in cultures where learning is not the norm, and companies do not grow when listening to customers and employees is not the norm. The firm can kill the message.

The firm can kill the messenger.

But, the firm will kill its people if they are not allowed to grow and succeed.

Statements About the Firm's Assets

- A culture sets norms about the relative value of a firm's assets. Firms succeed when they create an environment in which people succeed by using the firm's assets as efficiently and effectively as possible.

"It's not my money!" is the prevalent attitude in the fat firm. The result is usually obvious waste and fat. Often the waste helps the individual at the expense of the firm.

Sometimes the waste is mindless, bringing value to neither the firm nor the individual responsible for the waste.

A "cost-cutting" culture can underdeploy the firm's assets. People will not be as productive as they should be if they do not have the resources, tools, or training to do their jobs well.

The misallocation of the firm's assets is another source of fat. More than once, a promising product has languished due to underfunding while other highly persuasive product champions have gobbled up excessive resources for their products. The firm's assets can be misallocated across divisions, markets, business functions, and individuals.

CHAPTER 9:
THE WORKSTYLE OF THE FIRM

Values reflect what is important to the firm. Workstyle describes the actions and decisions of the firm. The Workstyle Wheel shows some of the many workstyle choices that define the firm's culture. Whereas extreme activity on any of the dimensions may be necessary in certain environments, extreme positions usually lead to inefficiency and ineffectiveness in the firm. Workstyles are neither good nor bad, just appropriate or inappropriate.

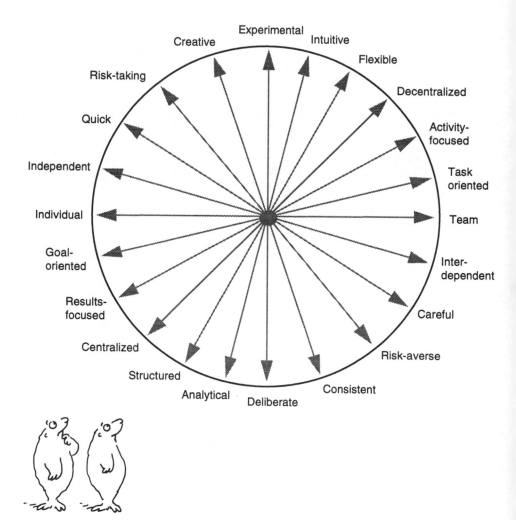

A firm's workstyle is characterized by who does the work and how it gets done.

Who Does the Work

The firm's culture specifies who makes the decisions and who accomplishes the firm's work. The culture resolves several dilemmas:

    Who makes the firm's decisions?

        Managers? Leaders? Empowered individuals? Teams? Empowered teams?

    Who does the firm's work?

        Managers? Leaders? Empowered individuals? Teams? Empowered teams? Another company?

The culture also helps decide when and under what conditions each of these alternatives is most appropriate. A firm gets fat when it makes poor "who" choices.

Teamwork can be very effective when all the team participants contribute in unique ways. On the other hand, teams that have free riders, role ambiguity or that lack creative, organizational, or implementation skills can be very ineffective.

Work in a firm requires insight and risk-taking. People will try to reduce the uncertainty and risk through discussion and sharing of responsibilities. But excessive meetings and consensus building can lead to a fat culture.

The number of meeting attendees grows quickly as the "like to know" crowd is added to the "need to know" participants.

How Work Is Accomplished

The firm's culture specifies how decisions are made and how the work gets done. It can encourage actions that come from the head, the heart, or the gut. One culture may be creative, intuitive and fast. Another may be structured, analytical and slow. Each style can be appropriate depending upon the circumstances.

Firms drift when they are poor at setting clear and unambiguous goals and objectives. Customers become confused about the value that they receive and employees become confused about their role in the organization.

Cultures that have an overly optimistic outlook or that set overly ambitious goals develop workstyles that encourage unrealistic strategies.

Workstyles that embrace myopic objectives usually lead to myopic decision making, behavior, and results.

Many markets are experiencing rapid change. Risk taking is essential for success in highly uncertain environments. A penalty culture freezes activity because everyone is afraid to take chances.

The workstyle of a firm can be rigid or flexible. A structured workstyle may be most appropriate when the firm is faced with a repetitive work situation. However, flexibility becomes key when the firm is frequently faced with a wide range of business situations. Adaptability is essential since markets and environments change continuously.

Speed of decisions and actions can be fast or slow. Each can be appropriate in the right circumstance.

Competitive cultures can be internally competitive as well as externally competitive. Competitive juices are best spent externally on the true competitor.

Many firms get highly politicized. Connections take precedence over competence. Decisions tend to be politically motivated as opposed to merit-based.

Firms are continuously bombarded with new ideas, and sometimes management fads drive a firm's actions. Excellence, Quality, Paradigm Shifts, Reengineering, High-Performance Teams, Workout—whatever today's or tomorrow's mantra is—it is likely to capture a partial view of the complex world of people and culture. These may be great ideas, which need to be incorporated into our general knowledge of management practice. However, there will always be situations where any one concept or practice will fail as a concept or in its implementation. It is always up to the people in the firm to use their own creative thinking and problem-solving skills to develop the most appropriate business solutions.

CHAPTER 10:
HOW CULTURES BECOME AND STAY FAT

Cultures evolve slowly. Values are articulated by the leaders and reinforced by the legends and celebrations. Workstyles are adopted when they have met the needs of the people and when they fit either the current culture or a desired future culture.

The firm's people are the only ones who can change a culture. They are the only ones who can make it fat. People create fat cultures when they are predisposed to fat or when they choose easy work. The principle of entitlement suggests that once fat takes hold of a culture, its impact accelerates.

The firm's environment dictates the extent to which fat can enter a culture. It is difficult to get fat in an unfavorable environment, whereas a favorable environment invites fat.

Cultures often stay fat because the firm is not aware that it has a fat culture. The firm is doing well. It is not measuring its vital signs, and there is no external benchmark indicating how well it could be doing.

This can also happen because the firm is aware that it has a fat culture, but the employees are enjoying its benefits. They prefer to maintain the status quo.

SUMMARY

The firm's culture is the DNA of the firm. It specifies the unwritten rules that help the firm define itself. It clarifies the importance of such dimensions as customer satisfaction, integrity, empowerment, appreciation, learning, agility, competition, corporate politics, fads, hard work, cost control, short-term financial focus, risk aversion, and team work. The firm's priorities are summarized by the firm's values and workstyle. Inappropriate values and workstyle create a fat culture.

A fat culture is not easy to change because it guides firm-wide behavior and it influences the choice of new hires. It has an inertia of its own that can only be affected by the people of the firm. This circuit—the culture influencing the firm's employees and the employees affecting the culture of the firm—places the firm's people in the position of determining whether the culture will be fit or fat in the future.

PART IV

The Processes
of the Fat Firm

A firm uses a multiplicity of processes to manage its activities and outcomes. The people of the firm create and work the processes.

There are processes that affect the firm's people, processes that affect its customers, and processes that affect its products and services. There are processes for:
- hiring, training, providing feedback, motivating, rewarding, and communicating,
- inventing products and services,
- obtaining raw materials, and for manufacturing and assembling the final products,
- creating market awareness, developing customer solutions, and delivering products and services, and for
- raising money, controlling costs, and measuring financial success.

How well processes are designed, how well they operate, and how they evolve over time determine whether a firm is fit or fat.

A Process Definition

Each of the firm's processes consumes *resources* and uses *activities* to produce *outputs*. For example, a production process may use raw materials, machines, and people as inputs. Activities include scheduling, setup, assembly, material flow, quality control, packaging, and cleanup. A packaged product, ready for shipping to the customer, is the output of the process. The relationship among resources, activities, and outputs is captured by *efficiency* and *effectiveness*. Efficiency is the ratio of activity to input, and effectiveness is the level of output for the level of activity.

Each process has a desired output. A process is highly *effective* when the appropriate activity and the right level of that activity are used to generate the output. An ineffective process wastes activity. A process is most *efficient* when the least amount of resource is consumed for a specified activity goal. An inefficient process wastes resources.

A process with high effectiveness and efficiency has high *productivity*. An inefficient process or an ineffective process harbors fat.

There are two more process components that can contribute to fitness or fat in a process. They are scale and *linkage*, which define how a process fits in a firm's business.

All processes have scale. Heavy processes use a lot of input and deliver a lot of output. Light processes use little input and deliver little output. A process with appropriate scale is right-sized.

The numerous processes within a firm are linked. The output of one process usually serves as an input to another. This linkage can create coordination problems in terms of timing, scale, or incompatibility between the output of one process and the input of another process. The complexity involved in synchronizing processes increases geometrically with the number of processes that need to be linked.

CHAPTER 11:
A HIRING PROCESS ILLUSTRATION

Hiring is an example of a process that exists in every firm and is a good illustration of each of the primary process components.

The hiring process uses the recruiting budget and recruiters as inputs. Hiring activities can include developing a job profile, finding an applicant pool, interviewing, selecting, and attracting the candidates to accept offers. Hiring outputs can be measured in terms of the number of hires, the quality level of the new employees, and the percentage of good hires that are with the firm in five years.

Hiring Resources

The input to the hiring process can be just right, or it can be too large, too small, or inappropriate. Too much money may be budgeted for the required output, thus creating inefficiency and waste. Too little money may be budgeted, thus creating a process that does not have the scale to meet its output goals and objectives. Use of the wrong recruiters can weaken the process—if weak people are selected as recruiters, weak selections will be made. People tend to hire in their own image. They often eliminate candidates who pose a threat to them. Recruiters influence the profile of the candidates who "fit" with the organization.

163

Hiring Efficiency

If it is sufficient for a candidate to be interviewed by five people, increasing the number to ten adds waste. An efficient hiring process uses the best amount of hiring inputs such as time and money for the desired hiring activity. An inefficient hiring process consumes too much money and personnel time to accomplish applicant pool development, resume screening, interviewing, reference checking, final selection and candidate attraction. Too much input is required for the desired activity.

Hiring Activity

The right activity can include developing an up-to-date candidate profile, administering objective tests to see if a candidate can succeed in the job, checking references and using behavioral interviews. The wrong activity is defined in terms of its inability to produce the desired outcome.

Hiring Effectiveness

A hiring process is effective if the process activities produce desired results. Selecting activities wisely enhances the effectiveness of the hiring process. For example, job competency tests are more effective than interviews, referrals produce better candidates than unsolicited write-ins or newspaper advertising, and well-crafted postoffer attraction programs increase the acceptance rate. Ineffective hiring processes create few new hires relative to the investment in the recruiting activity.

Hiring Output

The hiring process needs to produce employees who can be successful in their jobs now and in the future. As job definitions change over time, the process needs to match the candidate's skills, knowledge, and ability to grow with the needs of the job. It is important to use growth potential in the hiring profile. A mismatch will create frustration for both the candidate and the firm now or in the future.

Quality hiring dominates quantity hiring. Firms occasionally rush to fill a vacant position quickly and fail to pay enough attention to quality. This "warm-body" hiring is a common source of poor hiring output.

Hiring Scale

The scale of a hiring process can be too large, too small, or just right. An efficient and effective hiring process can still have too little or too much output. Hiring may produce too many hires for the positions available or too few—this can easily happen if the hiring process is static and duplicates a good job done the prior year when the situation needed more or fewer people. The problem is neither effectiveness nor efficiency, just scale—there is too much or too little hiring being done in the organization.

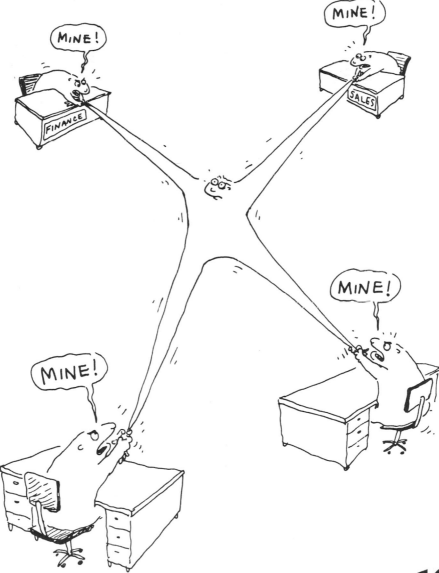

Hiring Linkage

The output of the hiring process serves as an input into other personnel processes such as training and development—and into the functional processes such as research, manufacturing, and selling. The hiring process provides the quality and quantity of personnel necessary to ensure that the firm can meet its objectives. It can also fail to provide the people that are required for the firm to succeed.

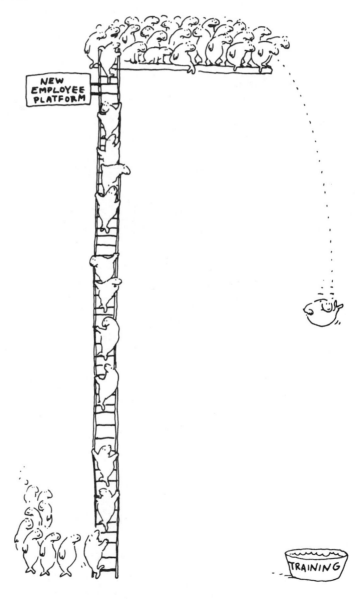

CHAPTER 12:
PROCESS COMPONENTS

The primary process elements—*inputs*, *activities*, and *outputs*, the relationships among them—*efficiency* and *effectiveness*, and the system dimensions—scale and linkage—provide an understanding of how processes work. It's not always easy to isolate fat in a process. Does a process use excessive resources? Is the activity wrong? Can a different activity produce output more effectively? Scale and linkage may be easy to judge. Efficiency may also be relatively easy to tackle. Effectiveness is likely to be the most difficult to assess since there is always room to improve.

The firm's processes are productive when *resources (inputs)* are used *efficiently* to create activity that leads to *output* in the most *effective* way. When any of these components misfires, then the process can contain fat.

We're overstaffed here at headquarters. Put them all into Sales.
Are you the Customer?
Are you the customer?
Are you the customer?

Resources

Too many resources applied to a productive process will produce too much output. Otherwise, the resource will get frittered away through either efficiency losses, the wrong activity, low effectiveness, or the wrong output.

Too much resource is not the only source of fat. The available resource may not be the most appropriate for the process.

Overallocation of resources to a process can occur with a powerful process owner.

Efficiency

Efficient processes use the least amount of resource to generate a desired level of activity. *Inefficient* processes are fat processes because they generate insufficient activity for the committed resources. Inefficiencies occur in several ways. Redundant or unnecessary activities produce waste. Uncoordinated activities create confusion. Activities that are slow waste time.

Sometimes, the output is unaffected by removing redundant process components.

Excessive activity is wasteful.

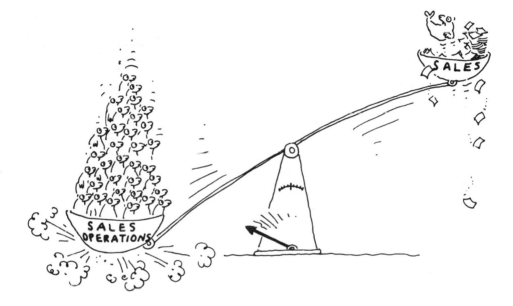

Lack of coordination creates inefficiency.

Slow activity is inefficient.

Activity

A great deal of process redesign focuses on identifying and eliminating wasteful activities from processes. The activities may not be needed because they duplicate other activities, serve no useful purpose, or because they are not the best for the desired process outcome.

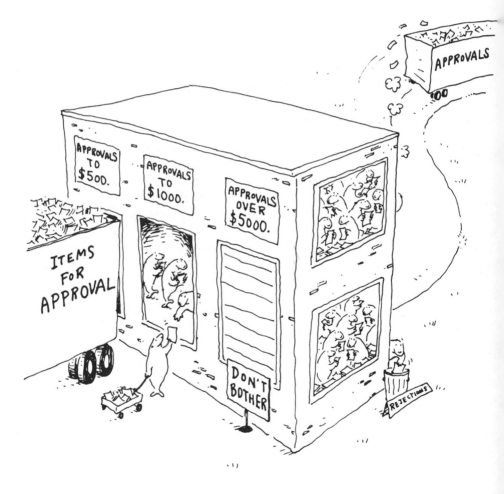

As organizations grow in size and complexity, it is difficult to have a complete picture of the whole organization. People tend to focus on their own limited domain in which they make decisions that appear the best for them. For the firm as a whole, one person's "must-have" becomes another person's burden that prevents him from doing what's really needed.

Some activities have immediate impact. Severe cost cutting is one of them. Essential activities can get overlooked in the haste to achieve a quick fix.

As departments get layered on top of one another, firms can have trouble with simple customer requests—the multiplicity of contact points and the lack of coordination across them creates waste and fat.

People can erect barriers to protect or insulate themselves. The cost, though, is lack of communication and synergy.

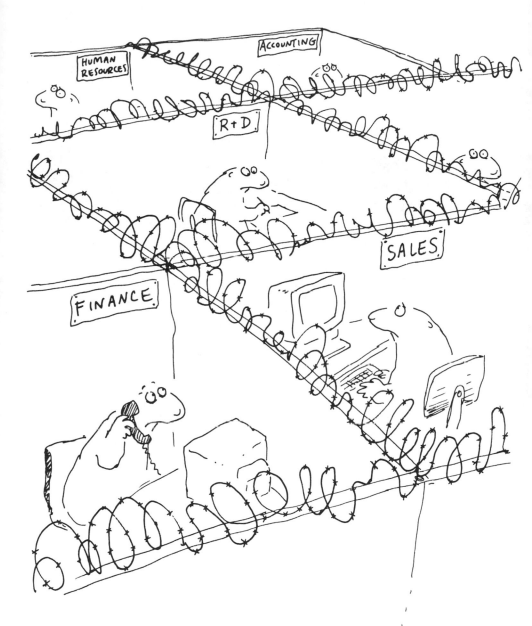

Effective processes use just the right activity for the desired output. Processes are ineffective when too much or the wrong activity is used for the results that are obtained.

A process is more effective when it works smarter, not harder.

More activity does not always produce proportionately more output. There can come a point when additional activity can actually diminish output. Project overstaffing is one example of this phenomenon. Advertising wearout is another example.

Overenthusiasm can lead to overkill.

A lack of a clear direction or miscommunication can also create an ineffective process.

Output

A process may not have sufficient output. It may be sufficient but lack quality. Or it may not be relevant or meaningful, such as a product that no one wants.

Process output can be low simply because the firm set its goals too low.

Scale

A heavy process uses too many resources and produces too much output. A light process uses too few resources and produces too little output.

Frequently, heavy processes result when an individual or a group of individuals feel that they can gain personally from the prominence of a process.

Process champions have a tendency to continually raise the prominence of their processes. The perceived importance of the process drives up its scale. Before long the process becomes too heavy. Too many resources are consumed. The firm doesn't know what to do with all of the output.

Light processes usually don't have a process champion or, if they do, they are unable to generate sufficient interest in the process.

Linkage

All of the processes in a firm are linked. The output of one process frequently serves as an input to another. Process linkage can create coordination problems and reduce productivity.

Many processes use inputs from diverse business functions or different groups within a department. A lack of coordination or linkage can lead to waste.

Occasionally, process enhancements which appear to boost output only add to waste because a preceding step cannot provide sufficient input, or a subsequent step cannot use the output fast enough.

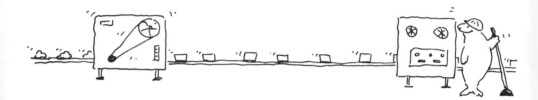

A functional organization with poor cross-functional linkages will produce undesirable results.

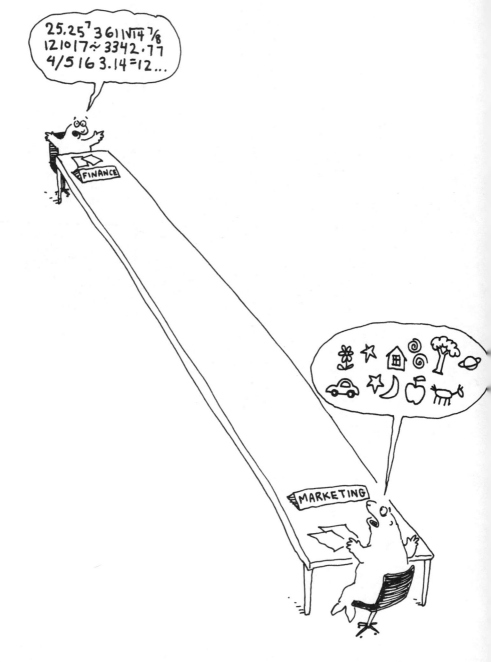

CHAPTER 13:
HOW PROCESSES GET FAT

Fit processes are flexible and evolve to meet the needs of the company. Fat processes undermine the potential success of the firm. Processes are fat at inception, they evolve into fat due to a lack of internal discipline, or they become fat because of external, environmental factors.

Process Creation

Sometimes people create nonessential or unnecessary processes. When this happens they have created fat for the life of the process. The process adds little value except in providing temporary security or satisfaction to the creators or process participants.

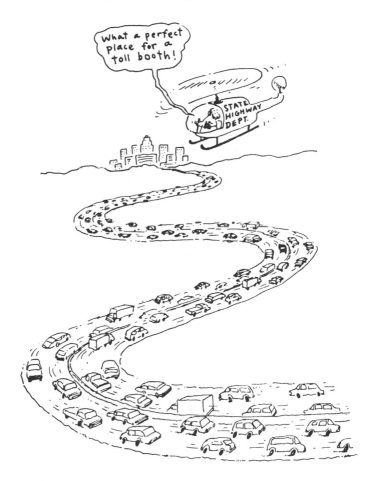

At other times, useful processes are designed poorly. After an initial shake-out and adjustment phase, they may still operate inefficiently and ineffectively. When process components are measurable, continuous improvement is more likely.

However, even in these cases the process may continue to stagnate because the process champions are not aware that their process has been poorly designed or they may just be blocking any improvement attempt.

Process Evolution

Processes can get fat, inch by inch, due to neglect and lack of discipline. This becomes more likely when it is difficult to measure the process. Process measurement enhances process awareness.

Process owners may not be paying attention to the process or process scale may be a surrogate for influence and power within the firm.

Processes may be well designed, but they fail when it comes to implementation and execution. Frequently, the wrong person or an inappropriate team is selected for the implementation. Design skills and implementation skills are not always the same.

Process discipline is hard work. Sometimes process owners opt for easy work. Easy work can lead to fat processes.

EASY WORK

HARD WORK

Environmental Factors

Processes that are appropriate for one time and place can become obsolete in the face of a changing environment.

An innovative competitor can render a process obsolete.

Technology can make processes obsolete.

Changing customer tastes are frequently at the root of process obsolescence.

CHAPTER 14:
WHY FAT PROCESSES SURVIVE

The firm's people and culture sustain fat processes. The process owners may not be aware that their process is fat. They may not want to improve a suboptimal process. Or, the firm's culture may accept or even nourish mediocre processes. Things are going fine. The firm is achieving its objectives. Why change anything?

People

People create processes. They are the only ones that can improve them. Why wouldn't the firm's employees want their processes operating at peak performance? Because there are times when their motivation, their lack of capabilities, or their values and attitudes can conflict with process productivity.

Motivators

People's need for survival, power, achievement, social affiliation, and ego gratification can hinder process improvement.

Capabilities

Processes can remain flat when their owners lack the leadership, management, or execution capabilities to make improvements.

Values and Attitudes

People can nourish fat processes through complacency. Their values and attitudes have an immediate impact on the processes in which they participate.

Culture

The firm's culture is a very powerful force. Processes become
intertwined with the culture. Over time a process change may
require a culture change. Rigid, dogmatic cultures that are heavily
invested in history and status quo will sustain weak and outdated
processes.

A firm's culture is guided by its values and is reflected in its workstyle. Cultures which value innovation and improvement and workstyles that are adaptive will inspire process improvement. Rigid values and workstyles lead to fat processes.

Workstyle and values are communicated through the firm's heroes, its legends, its myths, and its reward structures. Processes that are tightly associated with a legend may survive longer than needed.

SUMMARY

A firm uses many processes to manage its activities and outcomes. A firm with an adaptive culture can achieve fitness by constantly evaluating its processes and striving to improve them. Fat processes slow the firm down. They use too much input, create inappropriate activity, or produce too little output. They can be inefficient or ineffective, and have inappropriate scale or infeasible linkage. Diagnosis is not always easy. Sources of fat can be elusive, and process champions often defend their creations.

PART V

The Fit Firm

Change Is the Fitness Secret

All firms, whether fat or fit, need to continually change to survive and succeed. Change is the fitness secret. Not any change— relevant change! Change includes upgrading people, adapting the culture, and revamping the processes. Change is needed to deal with new challenges. But change holds risk and uncertainty. That's what makes it hard work, not easy work. The fit firm improves continuously to maintain its advantage. The fat firm needs drastic change to get fit.

Others need surgery.

Fitness is not just about COMFY, the fat firm in a favorable environment. COMFY's challenge is to get fit before the environment turns unfavorable. IFFY knows he's in trouble. There is no choice but to shape up. For SCRAPPY, the challenge is to stay fit or face death. TOUGHY may have the toughest challenge of all—to do the hard work necessary to stay fit when easy work tempts and beckons.

How does a firm change? It adapts and grows by changing its people and its culture. It succeeds by evolving its direction and strategy, its structure and its processes. Fitness is about evolution and adaptation.

A firm does not change for the sake of change.

It restructures to respond to new realities. It changes to identify, create, and seize new opportunities.

Change Can Be BIG BANG or Continuous

The firm can change completely or incrementally. Complete change is fast—Big Bang, zero-based, reengineering, start from scratch, total change.

Incremental change is evolutionary—constant improvement at all times, continuous, disciplined, daily fight to stay fit, Kaizen.

Complete change is surgery; continuous change is exercise. Each is possible and desirable under different circumstances. Dynamic market conditions may require a quick response from the firm. Fast change may be essential. In a stable environment, continuous change could be more desirable than total disruption.

The firm's people, culture, and processes all have different propensities for change. Typically, a complete change is more likely to occur for well-defined processes that have few linkages and dependencies. Processes are easier to change than people or culture. One can be done quickly; the others may take place incrementally and require years to do.

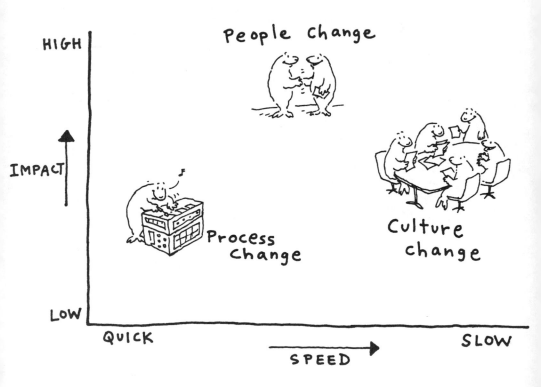

CHAPTER 15:
CHANGING PEOPLE

Sometimes the firm needs different people. At other times, it needs the same people, but with enhanced capabilities. The right people with the right capabilities still need to be motivated to perform and align their energies with the firm—they need incentives and rewards. The organization needs to define roles and responsibilities for its people in order to achieve its objectives.

Four processes can change the people of the firm: selection, development, reward, and organization.

Selection

Selection is choosing who gets assigned to tasks, work groups, or jobs. Selection includes who gets hired into the company, who is promoted, who gets assigned to open positions, and who is asked to leave a company. The firm's work is done by its people. Change the people, and the quality of the firm will change.

The selection process can weaken or strengthen the firm. It is driven by the people responsible for the selection and the firm's culture.

Fat results when people enhance their own position by hiring people weaker than themselves.

The firm gets stronger when better and better people are hired.

When a firm has weak people in a stagnant or decaying culture with obsolete processes, the solution is often a change at the very top. What is often needed is a different person—someone with no ties or personal links to the past.

Whether it is because of environmental forces or past flawed strategies, the fat firm often needs to selectively slim down its work force. The big mistakes tend to be made at the top. The heavy price is frequently paid by those in the ranks.

The selection or promotion of a person has an indirect effect—it communicates the values we want in the people.

Development

The firm and its people are energized and improved by personal
and professional growth. This growth comes from challenging
work, peer influence, and formal development programs. The firm
strengthens this process by recognizing growth as a priority and
sponsoring ways for people to expand their skills and knowledge.

The firm's culture is a powerful force in the development of the firm's people. The value system can define learning as a parameter of success, while the workstyle can encourage open communication, beneficial coaching, helpful mentoring, and constructive performance appraisals.

Reward

A firm's reward structure is a source of direction and motivation for the firm's people. The firm rewards its people for their commitment, work, and results. Rewards can effectively align a person's own motivators with the needs of the firm.

When opportunities for easy work and fat abound, the reward structure plays the role of increasing the attractiveness of hard work. It defines how the person and the firm win together.

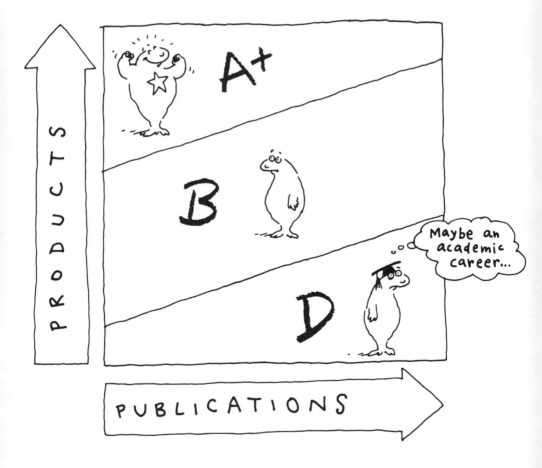

Rewards are both tangible and intangible. Tangible rewards include money and perks, such as trips and special events. Intangible rewards include appreciation, recognition, security, and a sense of belonging. Appreciative, consistent, and credible intangible rewards frequently have a greater impact on people than tangible rewards.

Support for a person's initiatives is a reward too. The firm allocates money and time to individuals to enable them to succeed at their work. The firm signals the importance of projects and people by how these resources are apportioned. Individuals can get resources to lighten their load, to build markets, or to grow their processes.

Reorganization

The firm can change its people by reorganizing its work. Work is modified when goals and objectives change. A firm that redefines tasks and activities places different expectations on individuals. For example, a firm may replace individual work with team work because customers want services that rely on several of the firm's capabilities.

To speed decision making and move decisions closer to where the information is, firms may move to create a flatter organization or devolve responsibilities to lower levels in the organization.

Reorganizing for fitness means eliminating activities that hinder the purpose of the firm.

CHAPTER 16:
CHANGING CULTURE

Only people can change a firm's culture. People update cultures by establishing a vision of the culture, communicating the desired values and workstyle constantly and consistently, incorporating the desired culture into their own actions, and rewarding the behaviors that reinforce the culture.

Establish a Vision of the Culture

Cultures are expressed and adapted constantly. Decisions are made, successes are celebrated, values are expressed, and workstyle choices are reinforced. Whether a firm is fat or fit, the challenge is to define the dominant cultural vision that needs to be sustained or revised. Is it focus on the customer? Is it appreciation for the firm's people? Or is it that increasing customer diversity dictates a more decentralized workstyle? The vision directs the cultural revision.

Communicate Preferred Values and Workstyle

The cultural vision of the company needs to be communicated repeatedly, consistently, and convincingly. It is communicated by the leaders of the firm in their public statements. It is communicated by the managers of the firm when they coach and mentor. It is communicated by all the people in the firm in their daily activities and in interactions with others. Fit legends and fit heroes are celebrated. Fit values and workstyles become part of the firm's muscle memory.

While the fit values and workstyles are celebrated, fat values are challenged and discouraged.

Incorporate Preferred Values and Workstyle Into Actions

Cultures change when people "walk the talk." If the firm's people do not live the fit culture, then the culture will not stay fit for long.

Well thought-out, concerted action needs to follow problem recognition.

A firm's communications and actions must have integrity. Cynicism results when words and actions are not consistent. When they are synchronized, the values get stronger and are propagated throughout the organization.

Stuffing distribution channels with unsold products derives from a culture that places extreme value on meeting short-term objectives, no matter what the long-term costs. A better approach would be to understand why the customers are not buying the product.

Reward Behaviors That Support the Preferred Culture

The fit culture rewards fit actions. Firms celebrate values and workstyles that embody the culture. For a fat firm to become fit, new fit cultural paradigms have to be rewarded and the fat ones rejected.

If fitness demands open communication, then people with information and insight, whether favorable or unfavorable, are rewarded and not punished. Bad news is treated as a signal for change, not a reason to shoot the messenger.

Risk-taking is not punished. Mistakes help people learn and get better. This becomes a cultural belief.

CHAPTER 17:
CHANGING PROCESSES

Upgrading processes requires awareness, insight, and action. If the firm's survival is immediately threatened, the threat forces awareness. Awareness is an issue for the fat firm in a favorable environment– for COMFY. The last thing on COMFY's mind is to give up any of the trappings of success. Insight is needed to figure out how to proceed. Insight, though, is not enough. The fit firm is action-oriented and implements vigorously.

Awareness

The key to awareness is relentless self-assessment. Are the internal processes necessary and productive?

Internal self-assessment is not enough. The fit firm's self-assessment includes understanding and paying attention to evolving customer needs and environmental forces.

Insight

Awareness about improvement opportunities has to be followed by insight to determine the best course of action. Some processes need to be enhanced, others eliminated, and still others may need a complete rethink.

Process redesign frequently involves cost reduction, where the focus is on identifying and eliminating redundant activities and steps. At other times, the output objective, such as timeliness, is enhanced.

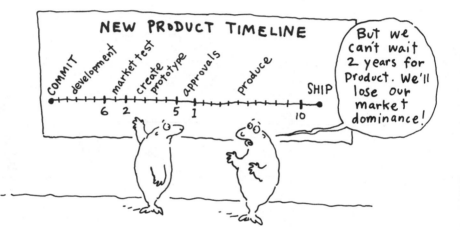

Sometimes, the process is completely unnecessary.

But at other times, a paradigm shift is required.

A focus on output—more, better, or different output—has been and will continue to be fertile ground for process innovation. Firms have discovered the value of process redesign for efficiency gains. Fit firms are likely to pursue more effectiveness enhancements in the future.

Action

Awareness and insight add up to very little without action. A new or upgraded process is designed based on insight. Action follows insight. Successful implementation requires the acceptance and support of process participants.

Sometimes the action necessary becomes clear by just looking at the problem.

Successful implementation goes well beyond just having a good plan. Success is really 10 percent inspiration and 90 percent implementation.

CHAPTER 18:
CHANGING THE FIRM

The fit firm upgrades its processes, adapts its culture, and grows
its people. Processes are redesigned for efficiency and effectiveness.
A new culture is imagined and then created through words,
actions, and rewards. People are selected, developed, rewarded,
and organized. Direct actions have indirect consequences. A new
person brought in to revamp an ailing division will undoubtedly
impact its culture, which in turn will influence the division's

There is a relationship between the source of fat and the change agent that is best suited to fix it.

Some change agents work for processes, others for people, and still others for culture. Some are more appropriate for a fast change, others are better for continuous improvement.

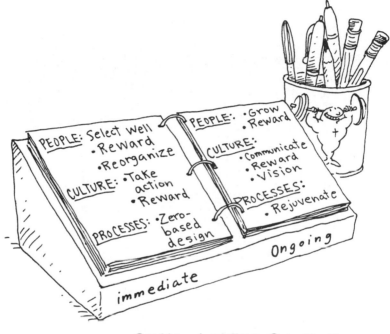

DESK ACCESSORY FOR
THE FIT MANAGER

The Fitness Advisory

All firms, either fat or fit, need to continually adapt to be fit in the future. The antifat treatment and its urgency depends on the success of the firm and the environment in which it competes. TOUGHY, COMFY, SCRAPPY, and IFFY face different challenges. SCRAPPY and TOUGHY are both fit. They have the right people doing the right things.

TOUGHY, the fit firm in a favorable environment

COMFY, the fat firm in a favorable environment

IFFY's top people need change, COMFY's need renewal. COMFY needs to become aware of the possible dangers he faces. TOUGHY has to continue strengthening his culture, COMFY needs to reverse the slide. SCRAPPY, with little room for error, needs to focus on making his processes better and better.

SCRAPPY, the fit firm in an unfavorable environment

IFFY, the fat firm in an unfavorable environment

The TOUGHY Advisory

TOUGHY is in an enviable position—fit in a favorable environment. Staying fit, though, can be harder than getting fit.

The firm's people created TOUGHY's success. TOUGHY achieved success by aligning the success of the firm's people with the success of the firm. TOUGHY keeps the key threat of creeping entitlement at bay by rewarding the necessary hard work and making the easy work culturally unacceptable. The other threat—a drastic shift in markets or technology—is dealt with through a culture of risk-taking and innovation.

The COMFY Advisory

COMFY is fat in a favorable environment—successful and probably unaware of the danger ahead if the environment turns. There is little incentive to change anything right now. Things are going well and everyone is enjoying the benefits of the fat. The fat is growing in the people, culture, and processes. It's hard to get rid of because it involves the firm's leaders and decision makers. A serious threat may be the only thing that can warn COMFY and arrest the slide to IFFY. COMFY needs the renewal that is frequently brought about by the untainted view of an outsider at or near the top. The challenge is to see as fat what the insiders view as their right.

The SCRAPPY Advisory

SCRAPPY is fit in an unfavorable environment. In this firm, the people and culture are strong. SCRAPPY is continually improving processes and using skills to shape customer needs and markets of the future. At the same time, Scrappy anticipates changes in the external environment and adapts speedily. But there is little room for error. There is no fat to cut if things turn unfavorable.

The IFFY Advisory

IFFY is fat in an unfavorable environment and needs a transformation, fast. The first place to look? At top management. They got IFFY into this position. But they have too many vested interests to bring about the drastic changes needed. A change at the top is the first step in setting a new course for IFFY, a course with a new culture and new processes.

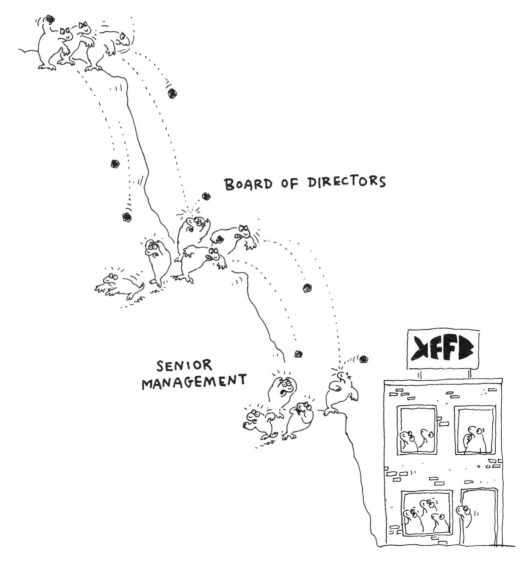

STOCKHOLDERS

BOARD OF DIRECTORS

SENIOR MANAGEMENT

It's the People

A new elegant strategy, a new state-of-the-art structure, a redesigned process—these are all useful for success. But processes and structures and strategies come from the people of the firm. The firm's people drive the firm's success or failure. They create the firm's problems and they resolve them. The firm's people shape its culture daily, and they continuously create and adapt its processes.

People make the firm. They make it successful or they make it fat. People make a fat firm fit and people keep a fit firm fit.